THE WALLASE BUS

By

TB MAUND FCIT

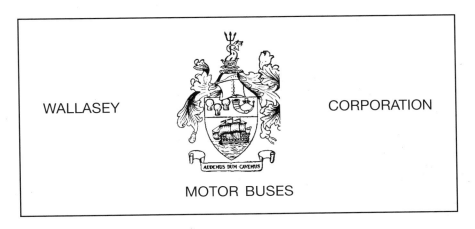

WALLASEY   CORPORATION

MOTOR BUSES

Design & Origination: Ian Boumphrey - Desk Top Publisher

Printed by: Printfine Limited, Liverpool

Published by: Ian & Marilyn Boumphrey
"The Nook"
Acrefield Road
Prenton
Wirral L42 8LD

ISBN 1-899241-05-1

Errata:
Pages 50 & 56
⁹ Should read ½
Page 55
Note U should read:
14, 22-3, 25-6 & 30
Page 56, caption 3 should be
5¼ miles

Front Cover:
Top: *One of Wallasey's first AEC buses which entered service in 1920.*
*Bottom: A contrast in styles. Leyland PD1 No. 25, new in 1948 but with a Metropolitan-Cammell body
virtually identical to those of a decade earlier, stands alongside 1959 Atlantean No. 4 with a very
different body by the same manufacturer. Note the small frame on the cab side of No. 25 which
was used to advertise band concerts in Vale Park. A somewhat larger frame is fitted behind the cab
on the Atlantean.*

**PRICE
£5.95**

Corporation Motor Buses.

SEASOMBE AND HARRISON DRIVE ROUTE.

From SEACOMBE FERRY TO HARRISON DRIVE.

Mondays to Fridays—

Seacombe Ferry leave 8-30 a.m., 8-50, 9-10, 9-30   9-50, 10-10 and every 30 minutes until 11-40, 12-0 noon, and every 20 minutes until 5 p.m., and every 10 minutes until 7-20, 7-40, and every 20 minutes until 10-40 p.m.

Saturdays.—As Monday to Friday until 12 noon, 12-10 p.m., 12-20, 12-30 and every 10 minutes until 10-40.

Sundays.—9-57 a.m., 10-12, and every 15 minutes until 1-27 p.m., 1-40, and every 20 minutes until 10-0, 10-27 p.m.

From HARRISON DRIVE to SEACOMBE FERRY—

Mondays to Fridays.—

Harrison Drive leave 9-50 a.m., 10-13, 10-43, 11-13, 11-40, and every 20 minutes until 4-40 p.m., 5-0, 5-20, and every 10 minutes until 7-0, and every 20 minutes until 10-40 p.m.

Saturdays.—As Monday to Friday until 11-40 a.m., 12-0 noon, 12-20 p.m., and every 10 minutes until 10-40 p.m.

Sundays.—9-35 a.m. 10-5, and every 15 minutes until 1-35 p.m., 1-50, 2-0, and every 20 minutes until 10-20 p.m.

SEACOMBE AND BIRKENHEAD ROUTE.
(Run conjointly with Birkenhead Corporation Motors).

From SEACOMBE FERRY to CHARING CROSS.

Mondays to Fridays—

Seacombe Ferry, leave 7-40 a.m., 8-20, 9-0, 9-40, 10-20, 11-0, 11-40, 12-20 p.m., 1-0, 1-40, 2-0, 2-20, 2-40, 3-0, 3-20, 3-40, 4-0, and every 20 minutes until 10-40.

Saturdays.—As Monday to Friday until 2-0 p.m., 2-15, 2-30, 2-45, and every 15 minutes until 11-0 p.m.

Sundays.—1-40 p.m., 2-0, 2-20, 2-40, 3-0, 3-15, and every 15 minutes until 11-0 p.m.

From CHARING CROSS to SEACOMBE FERRY.
Mondays to Fridays—

Charing Cross leave 8-0 a.m., 8-40, 9-20, 10-0, 10-40, 11-20, 12-0 noon, 12-40 p.m., 1-20, 2-0, 2-20, 2-40, 3-0, 3-20, 3-40, 4-0, 4-20, and every 20 minutes until 11-0 p.m.

Saturdays.—As Monday to Friday until 1-20 p.m., 1-37, 1-52, and every 15 minutes until 10-52, 11-5 p.m.

Sundays.—2-0 p.m., 2-20, 2-37, 2-52, 3-7, 3-22, and every 15 minutes until 10-52 p.m.

LISCARD AND BIRKENHEAD ROUTE.
(Run conjointly with Birkenhead Corporation Motors).

From LISCARD VILLAGE to CHARING CROSS.
Mondays to Fridays—

Liscard Village, leave 7-35 a.m., 8-5, 8-35, 9-5, 9-35, 10-5, 10-35, 11-5, 11-35, 12-5 p.m., 12-35, 1-5, 1-30, 1-50, 2-10, 2-30, and every 15 minutes until 10-10, 10-35 p.m.

Saturdays.—As Monday to Friday until 1-50 p.m., 2-5, 2-20, 2-35, and every 15 minutes until 10-35, 10-55 p.m.

Sundays.—2-30 p.m., 2-50, 3-5, 3-20, 3-35, 3-50, and every 15 minutes until 10-35 p.m.

From CHARING CROSS to LISCARD VILLAGE.
Monday to Fridays—

Charing Cross, leave 8-5 a.m., 8-35, 9-5, 9-35, 10-5, 10-35, 11-5, 11-35, 12-5, 12-35, 1-5, 1-30, 1-50, 2-10, 2-30, and every 20 minutes until 10-10, 10-35, 11-0 p.m.

Saturdays.—As Monday to Friday until 1-30, p.m., 1-45, 2-0, 2-15, and every 15 minutes until 11-0 p.m.

Sundays.—2-10 p.m., 2-30 2-45, 3-0, 3-15, 3-30, and every 15 minutes until 10-30 p.m.

The Intermediate and arrival times on all routes are approximate only.

The Corporation reserve the right to alter, without notice, the running and arrival of the buses. The Buses of the Corporation may be hired for the conveyance of private parties, etc.

TRAMWAYS DEPARTMENT,

SEAVIEW ROAD, WALLASEY.

H. H. LINCOLN, A.M-I.Mech.E.,

[Taken from a Wallasey Guide 1927-8]

General Manager

INTRODUCTION

The former County Borough of Wallasey was formed by the intergrowth of a number of separate villages, Seacombe, Poulton, Wallasey and Liscard. New Brighton and Egremont were developed as desirable residential areas and resorts from the 1830s while Leasowe and Moreton were added in 1928 and Saughall Massie in 1933. Bounded on the east by the River Mersey, on the north by the Irish Sea and on the south by the Wallasey Pool, converted into docks from 1847 onwards, Wallasey was rather isolated from its neighbours and, indeed, the name is said to have evolved from the Celtic Walleas Eye, meaning Isle of Strangers.

Three ferries operated across the river to Liverpool from New Brighton, Egremont and Seacombe and the Wallasey Local Board obtained control of them in 1861, the same year that the first service of horse drawn omnibuses, between Seacombe and New Brighton, began. They must have gone via Liscard Village as Seabank Road, the direct route, was not then built. Horse tramways were proposed in 1870 but it was not until 30th June 1879 that a line was opened from Seacombe to Field Road, Upper Brighton. The tramway and omnibus services were merged into the Wallasey United Tramway & Omnibus Co. Ltd. in 1888 and the Urban District Council took over the tramways from 31st March 1901. The Council then constructed four electric tram routes, all connecting Seacombe with New Brighton which were opened between 1902 and 1911.

Wallasey achieved borough status in 1910 and became a county borough three years later. Parliamentary powers to run motor buses were obtained in 1920 and a service between Seacombe ferry and Harrison Drive via Manor Road and St. Hilary Brow commenced running on 3rd April 1920. Routes across the docks into Birkenhead were started jointly with Birkenhead Corporation in 1921 and buses were used to augment the trams at very busy times. Services to Moreton were commenced on the day the area was incorporated into Wallasey - 1st April 1928. Powers to run trolleybuses were obtained in 1927 but these were never used. As the tram tracks wore out, it was decided to replace the trams by buses and the busy Seabank Road route, which was hampered by much single track, was successfully changed over on 20th January 1929. The other routes followed and the last trams ran at midnight on 30th November 1933.

Like the trams before them, Wallasey's buses were painted a pale shade of yellowish green usually referred to locally as 'sea green'. However this was derived from an old tale about someone asking what colour the trams should be painted and being told to 'see Greene', the manager in the early days. The official description was 'primrose green and cream'.

Most of the bus services were timed to connect with the boats at Seacombe ferry from where there was a 10-minute service to and from Liverpool for most of the day. All the principal routes ran every 10 minutes, too. At peak hours, the departure of the buses from Seacombe was a fine sight to behold. The buses would set down any incoming passengers at the ferry building, then run round to the south side and reverse into the allotted stands under the guidance of the conductor. Once all the passengers had come off the boat, the inspector would blow his whistle and up to 15 buses would depart simultaneously, the whole procedure being repeated 10 minutes later.

During the 1930s, two new open air bathing pools, one of Olympic standards, and a two-mile promenade extension, attracted thousands of visitors to New Brighton and Wallasey. Despite the lack of amenities, thousands also went to Moreton Shore. The bus service became highly profitable and large sums were contributed to the rate fund. Fares were reduced progressively until 1935 and remained at that level for the next 16 years. This was the golden age of New Brighton and of the bus service. When war broke out, the service was drastically curtailed to save petrol and rubber and, during the grim air raid period of 1940-42, many people moved away from the town. As many as 25 of Wallasey's buses then went on war service to Wrexham, returning in a somewhat battered state after the end of the war.

The five years between the end of the war and 1950 saw the greatest volumes of traffic carried as there was a pent up demand for travel after so many years of austerity. In the peak year 1949-50 36,590,009 passengers were carried and the buses ran 3,182,882 miles. New routes were started into Birkenhead and the Wirral countryside but costs were rising inexorably and fares started to rise in 1951. Lacking the intensive industrial traffic of Birkenhead, and with a much higher car ownership figure, the Wallasey bus undertaking was soon losing money, higher fares discouraging travel by bus even more. The fleet contracted from a maximum of 110 buses just after the war to 64, several of which were out of service.

On Merseyside, Wallasey was a pioneer of what would now be called minibuses, small buses being used to penetrate the residential areas as early as 1962, nearly a quarter of a century before minibuses were generally adopted for this role. In 1966, consultants were engaged to plan a new network but the data was wrongly interpreted and the introduction of 'the computerised bus service' on 13th February 1967 was followed by a storm of protest, many of the old facilities having to be reinstated after a few weeks. Decline continued and in 1968-69 only 14,861,771 passengers were carried over 2,118,965 miles.

The undertaking was transferred, along with those of Liverpool and Birkenhead, to the Merseyside Passenger Transport Executive on 1st December 1969. Wallasey and Birkenhead became the Wirral Division and, for a time, the buses were painted in a combined livery of Wallasey cream and Birkenhead blue.

1-2 The three electric tram routes, opened between Seacombe and New Brighton in 1902, did not serve Poulton or Wallasey Village and the Council permitted R & J Evans, hauliers of 1 Matthew Street, Seacombe to run a service between the ferry and St. Luke's Church, Poulton in 1907; it was extended along Breck Road to Harrison Drive on 8th February 1908. The four buses, painted red and carrying the rather grand title 'Seacombe, Poulton and Wallasey Omnibus Co.' were bought second-hand from London. The upper picture shows two buses standing by St. Luke's Church with Poulton Hall in the background while the lower one shows a bus in Breck Road which remained narrow and partly rural until the 1940s. The buses were withdrawn when the trams were extended in 1910-11.

T B Maund collection

3

3-4 Wallasey's first Corporation buses were six solid-tyred AECs with 32-seat bodies made by E & A Hora. The seats were wooden and the massive overhang behind the rear axle must have made them very difficult to handle, especially when fully loaded. The wooden destination board at the front and the route boards along the sides had to be turned over at each terminus. No. 5 is seen in Wallasey Village at the top of Leasowe Road while the location of the picture of No. 6 is uncertain. Four extra passengers could be carried alongside the driver.
T G Turner collection

4

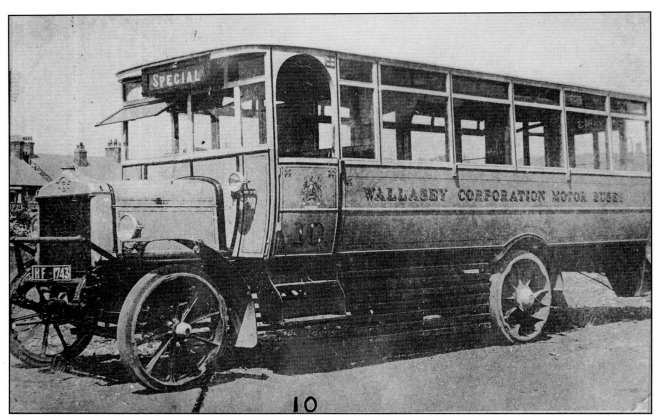

5 When more buses were needed in 1922, Wallasey Corporation bought four more AECs second-hand from Liverpool Corporation for £450 each. They were almost identical to the 1920s buses except that they had roller blind destination indicators instead of boards. They were numbered 7-10 and, although it was strictly speaking, illegal, they were re-registered in Wallasey. No. 10, HF 1743, was originally KB 1979. Liverpool had bought these buses in 1919 to help out their trams, many of which were in urgent need of repair because of wartime neglect. All the AECs were withdrawn in 1926. No. 10 saw further service in Wiltshire, lasting until 1931.

T G Turner collection

6 During the General Strike of May 1926, a few trams and buses were manned by volunteers though there many violent scenes in efforts to stop them running. Bus No. 3 is seen leaving Seacombe ferry with wire mesh protecting the windscreen and a policeman riding on the step. Note the very narrow wheels which typified these early buses. Note also the Ford model T van behind and the elderly Beardmore taxis on the left.

T B Maund collection

7

7-8 The summer service between the top of Harrison Drive and the Shore started on 12th July 1924 and, the following year, the Corporation tried out this Leyland Leveret PLA1 demonstrator. Passengers board (above) outside where Windsor's motor showroom now stands and (lower) at the Shore where the animated scene with chalets and tents is so different from that of today. Note the AEC bus almost hidden on the left and the boy with a towel round his neck who is wearing an old-style Oldershaw school cap.

Leyland Motors

8

9

9-10 The Leyland PLSC Lion was one of the most successful buses of the 1920s, over 4000 being built of which some were still in service in 1950 - though not in Wallasey. Powered by a 5.1-litre Leyland four-cylinder petrol engine, these buses were the first on purpose-designed passenger chassis with a lower floor than on earlier models. The bodies, too, were built by Leyland, with stretched canvas roofs over a tongue-and groove wooden structure. The saloon was divided into two compartments, smokers being confined to the rear. No. 1 which entered service in March 1926 was photographed near Leyland before delivery.
Leyland Motors

10

11-12 Although Wallasey had only 10 Lions, there were three variations in body design. Nos. 1-5 had the rear destination blind in the window whilst 6-10 had it on the roof. Nos. 6-7 had a forward entrance and rear emergency door while the others had a rear entrance. No. 4 stands in Virginia Road on the hourly No. 9 service to Moreton via Warren Drive and Grove Road, introduced in 1930 and not revived after wartime suspension. Note the 'Hackney Carriage 31 seats' sign and the spare wheel stowed at the rear. The queue barriers are as yet unroofed. In the lower picture, No. 7 stands at Seacombe on the Charing Cross service. The conductor is wearing his white 'summer top' but not the driver; double breasted tunics were worn until the 1960s. This was the last Lion to run for, after conversion to an emergency ambulance in 1939, it was reconverted to a bus and ran on a special contract service to Neston until 1944. An attempt to preserve No. 8 unfortunately failed but parts of it were used in restoring Ribble Lion No. 295 which is now in the Manchester Museum of Transport.

D S Deacon

12

13

13-14 Wallasey did not buy any Leyland Leverets which were considered too small for the Harrison Drive shuttle service. Instead, in 1927, they bought a Karrier JKL with a Hall Lewis body resembling those on the Lions. The general manager, H H Lincoln, designed the body with four removable panels on the nearside so that it could become a semi-toastrack in the summer and load and unload very quickly. No. 11 is seen loading at the top of Harrison Drive and again at the shore end on what appears to be a chilly day.
D Randall/D S Deacon

14

15

15 The Karrier JKL No. 11 was rarely seen with its four detachable nearside panels in position as it was used out of season only when there was a serious bus shortage. It had a Karrier 4-cylinder 6-litre engine and was low-geared. Its last appearance in winter service was in 1933-34 when it worked on route 9 from New Brighton to Moreton via Grove Road. It became a canteen when war broke out but the body caught fire and it was last seen as an auxiliary fire tender, parked on the upper floor of Seacombe ferry car park in 1941.
T G Turner collection

16

16-17 Two three-axle Karrier WL6/1 single deckers, with dual entrances and 40-seat Hall Lewis bodies went into service in August 1927. This was the age of the six-wheeler which was not to last long as there were many mechanical problems and excessive tyre wear. Nos. 12-13 were powered by six-cylinder Dorman 6JUL 6.59-litre engines and, because of their low build were nicknamed 'the snakes'. No. 12 is seen at Seacombe ferry and No. 13 in Groveland Road, the terminus of the Seacombe-Harrison Drive services until 24th December 1934. When new, all the six-wheelers had black waterproof covers over the rear wheels. The 'wavy' look of the lower picture is due to a camera fault.

D S Deacon

17

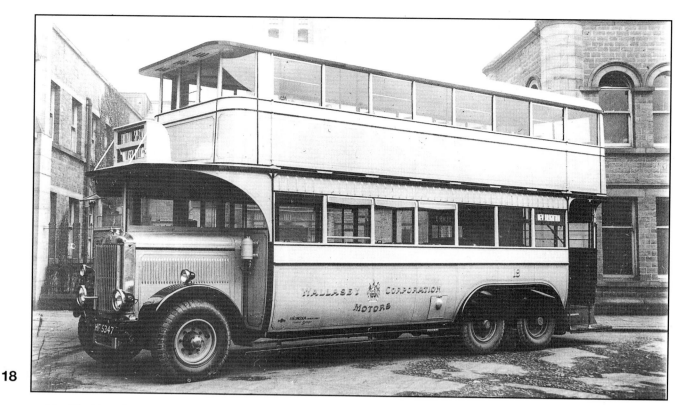

18

18-19 Six of these massive three-axle Karrier DD6 double-deck buses (14-19) entered service in June 1928. They had 66 seats, about the same as a tram, and were intended for the Seabank Road route when the trams were replaced. However, they were mechanically unreliable, all being returned to the works for attention. They consumed enormous quantities of oil and it is said that cans of oil were kept at Seacombe ferry for use in emergencies. The bodies, which tended to rattle vigorously, were by Hall Lewis, the predecessor of Park Royal. All the Karriers except No. 11 were withdrawn suddenly in August 1931 following a dreadful accident in King Street when the trap over the rear bogie of a double-decker gave way and a passenger fell through with fatal consequences. However, they were sold to Canvey & District Motor Transport Co. for whom they ran for several more years, No. 17 being withdrawn in 1937.

R Marshall collection/J F Higham

19

20-21 The all-Leyland Titan TD1 low-height double-deck bus revolutionised the bus industry and, in the early 1930s it was Wallasey's standard bus, six being bought in 1928 and 30 in 1929. The upper deck seats were arranged in rows of four, except the rear one which was for three and the gangway, which protruded into the lower saloon, was along the offside. Lower deck passengers were advised to lower their heads before leaving their seats. It had been hoped to have the first examples running for the inauguration of the Moreton services on 1st April 1928 but it was the 4th before they were ready. No. 20 is seen at Seacombe on its first day and No. 40 some years later at Virginia Road, New Brighton; the side destination indicators were added later and a route number box at the front only in 1931. *Leyland Motors/D S Deacon*

22 Leyland Titan TD1 No. 26 loads passengers at Seacombe ferry for New Brighton, with a similar bus in the background. The occasion was probably the first day of buses on the Seabank Road route - 20th January 1929 - when the second batch of Leyland Titans entered service. While Birkenhead Corporation and Crosville eventually enclosed the platforms and stairs of their TD1s, Wallasey sold theirs in 1936-37 in original condition. All except No. 33 were sold to the large Scottish operator, W. Alexander & Sons Ltd. for whom they ran much longer than in Wallasey. They were all enclosed at the rear and many were fitted with diesel engines.
courtesy M Jenkins

23

23-24 The centre picture symbolises the changeover from trams to buses. It is 1932 and the reconstruction of the Seacombe ferry terminal is underway. The trams, curtailed at Grove Road, are confined to the southern side of Victoria Place while the No. 6 bus has taken over the Church Street route, formerly served by the 'WD' tram and the section between Grove Road and New Brighton. In the lower picture, the bus is already using part of the new approach road and the cabmen's shelter awaits demolition.
M J O'Connor/ T B Maund collection

24

25

26

25 Rear view of a low-height Leyland Titan when new showing the staircase, under which a spare wheel was stored, leading to the offside upper deck gangway.
D S Deacon

26 The colonade at Seacombe ferry when new, before queue barriers were installed. Three Titans and a Lion are in position and the AEC can just be seen reversing in. White lines guide the buses but they needed repainting so often that metal studs were hammered in and many of them, indicating the route numbers of the services, are still in position in 1994 - sixty years later.
T B Maund collection

27 A busy holiday scene at the foot of Victoria Road, New Brighton with 1929 Leyland TD1 No. 21. The bus, which is standing on the track of the tram it has replaced, has no route number so the year is 1929 or 1930. Crowds are coming off the ferry pier and the Promenade Pier with its impressive domed pavilion is on the left.
Commercial post card

28 Leyland Titan TD1 No. 40 is seen again in Wallasey Road, heading towards Liscard Village, with the old market on the left and the end of St. Albans Road on the right. The road was widened in 1938 and Coronation Buildings built on the north side.
T G Turner collection

29 At least three open-staircase Titans are included in this line up of buses unloading in Rowson Street about 1935. Note how the route number box has been added. The building on the left is the Maris Stella Convent Girls' School. The disused tram track has not yet been lifted.
  C Garner collection

30 The Moreton, Bermuda Road terminus about 1929. Bermuda Road goes off to the right and Arrowe Lane (later Acton Lane) to the left. The back of the Wallasey boundary post can be seen just to the right of the bus. The Titan is about to depart for Seacombe ferry.
  T G Turner collection

31-32 Two views of Seacombe ferry terminal dating from 1934 show a variety of buses of the period. The parking spaces are still marked out in white paint. In the upper view the inspector has just blown his whistle and the 'camel' No. 56 on the Seabank Road service leads the exodus. Drivers can be seen entering the cabs of the two buses on the right. Open back Titans dominate the scene in the lower view, Nos. 22, 24 and 25 being identifiable. Two 1934 AEC Regents are on routes 1 and 2.

T G Turner collection/courtesy M Jenkins

33-34 The Associated Equipment Co. Ltd. (AEC) demonstrated their 'Regent' model to Wallasey Corporation in 1929 resulting in this bus with a Short Brothers body being purchased. Similar in many respects to the Leyland Titan, it had pairs of seats on the upper deck, headroom being given by a large hump in the roof. Inevitably No. 56 was nicknamed 'the camel'. The lower view, taken in Virginia Road, New Brighton on a busy summer day shows the rear platform and the curved glass corner panel upstairs and the 'ferry clocks' which were supposed to be set by the conductor to show the times of the boats at Seacombe and Egremont with which the bus connected. Note also the non-standard single destination indicator and the handrails which were white while those of the Titans were brown.

AEC/C Garner collection

35-36 In 1930 Wallasey Corporation adopted the practice of dividing quite small orders for new buses between two manufacturers. They also specified an additional front exit door and staircase to speed up unloading at Seacombe ferry. Nos. 57-59 were mechanically similar to the earlier Titans but the bodywork was by Davidson of Trafford Park, Manchester. The extra stairs resulted in the loss of eight seats so these buses seated only 48 passengers, less than a modern single-deck bus. The front exit was activated by the driver who leant out from the cab and pulled a lever fitted above the front bulkhead window. These buses were also the first to be equipped to show route numbers which were commenced on 1st January 1931 in both Wallasey and Birkenhead. In 1936, No. 58 was used in an experiment for running buses on compressed coal gas, in which Wallasey was a pioneer, several buses and municipal vans and lorries being converted during the war. Heavy steel tanks were fitted below the floor and it is shown being refuelled at the gas works in Gorsey Lane.

Leyland Motors/T B Maund collection

37

37 This picture shows the arrangement of the front exit and staircase on the first bus so equipped - No. 57. Coincidentally, Wallasey was to take delivery of 57 buses to this design between 1930 and 1936. Note also the ferry stoppage curtain peeping out above the first window. In tram days, flags were flown on the trolley rope to warn passengers that Egremont and/or New Brighton ferries were not running due to 'stress of weather'. The curtains on the buses worked like a roller blind and could be drawn half way down to indicate 'New Brighton Ferry Closed' in blue or all the way down to show also 'Egremont Ferry Closed' in red   *Leyland Motors*

38 The other half of the 1930 order went to Daimler in the form of three CF6 buses with similar Davidson bodies to Nos. 57-59. No. 61 is shown at the old Seacombe ferry terminal early in 1931. Note the old ferry clock tower, which housed hydraulic equipment for the goods lift, three trams on the loop and the three Titans which have not yet been fitted with route number boxes. The Daimlers were underpowered and were eventually relegated to part-day duties prior to withdrawal in 1937.

D S Deacon

39 The 1931 order was again for six buses and was divided between AEC and Leyland. Nos. 63-64 appear to have been the first diesel-engined buses to run in regular service on Merseyside; they were very unpopular because of their noise and smell and there were many letters of complaint in the press. Their bodies were built by Park Royal Vehicles, successors to Hall Lewis and the elaborate lining out and positioning of the fleet numbers behind the rear wheels suggests that the paint specification for the Karriers was used. No. 63 is seen at the Meadway stop in Belvidere Road. Note the standard Wallasey request stop sign in a wooden frame worded "Wallasey Corporation 'Buses Stop Here On Request" on a blue background.
D S Deacon

40

40-41 The other four 1931 buses, Nos. 65-68, were Leyland Titans, the last of the TD1 model, the bodies being supplied by Eastwood and Kenning (an ancestor of the Kenning motor group) who were successors to Davidsons. The front end treatment of the upper deck was most ungainly, appearing to have been added as an afterthought. The nearside view, taken before delivery, shows the front exit and staircase and also the strap across the rear platform which was placed in position by the conductor when the bus was full. In the offside view, No. 66 is seen in Warren Drive at the Grove Road junction. Note the time clock which had to be punched by the conductor to prove that the bus had not run early.
D S Deacon

41

42-43 Leyland and Daimler again shared the 1932 order. There were three Leyland Titan TD2s (69-71) and three Daimlers of the CP6 model (72-74) with fluid flywheels and preselector gearboxes delivered in March followed by a further three Titans in August (75-77). The body order went to English Electric and Wallasey Corporation was to buy 47 bodies of this design over the next five years. These buses were the first to have the nearside destination indicator over the door. The pictures, both taken at the Cambridge Road stop in Seabank Road show how identical bodies can sit differently on various chassis. The Leyland's front axle is slightly further forward and the short radiator is already dated. Note that the Leyland has an autovac on the front bulkhead into which petrol was pumped to run into the carburettor by gravity. The stop sign is a red compulsory stop where all buses stopped.

D S Deacon

43

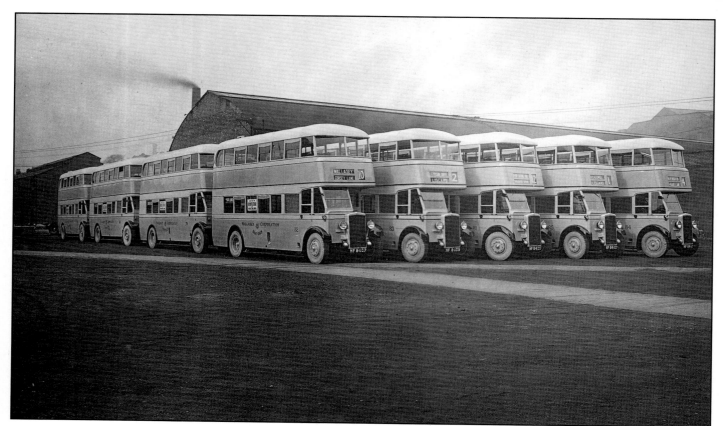

44 A total of 47 dual-entrance, double-staircase 48-seat bodies built by the English Electric Co. at Preston were purchased by Wallasey Corporation between 1932 and 1936. They comprised six AECs, eight Daimlers and 33 Leylands of three models. The March 1933 delivery of five Daimler CP6 and three Leyland TD2 were photographed before leaving the English Electric works. The five Daimlers (81-85) make up the front row with the three Leylands (78-80) behind. These were the last buses to have small destination equipment.
English Electric Co. courtesy J B Horne.

POSTING BOXES.

POSTING BOXES are affixed to Motor Buses on Mondays to Fridays (Bank Holidays excepted) as follows :—

	Route No.	From Seacombe Ferry at	Returning from New Brighton at
Via Seabank Road Route	1	9-25 p.m.	9-42 p.m.
Via Albion Street Route	5	9-20 p.m.	9-40 p.m.
Via Belvidere Road Route	6	9-10 p.m.	9-35 p.m.
Via Seaview Rd. and Warren Drive Route	16	9-10 p.m.	9-35 p.m.
Via Poulton and Marlowe Road Route	17	9-0 p.m.	9-30 p.m.
			From Bermuda Road
Via Seacombe and Moreton Route 4		9-0 p.m.	9-30 p.m.

This information was taken from a 1932 Wallasey Corporation Time Table and Fares booklet

45

45-46 These animated scenes in New Brighton date from about 1934. The upper picture shows crowds queueing for buses in Virginia Road where the 'cattle pens' are still open to the elements. Leyland Titan TD2 No. 70 is loading for Seacombe on the 17 route via Wallasey Village and Poulton Road while TD3 No. 90 passes, already well loaded for New Ferry. The lower view shows the Rowson Street stop in Victoria Road with one of the 1933 TD2s (78-80) on the No. 17 route followed by a 1933 Daimler of the 81-85 batch on the No. 8 route to Moreton (Bermuda Road). The open back Titan in the background is bound for New Ferry.

C Garner collection

46

47 The upper deck layout of the twin-staircase buses was not unlike that of front entrance buses still running today though the main staircase was, of course, at the rear. This interior view of 1932 Daimler No. 72 shows the well-upholstered seats and the half drop windows which were prone to jamming as the bodies flexed. These buses were 8.5in. narrower than modern vehicles, hence the rather cramped impression.
English Electric Co. Courtesy M Jenkins

Cheap Return Tickets by Ferry and Motor Omnibus

BETWEEN

Liverpool Stage and Moreton,	Liverpool Stage & New Brighton
via SEACOMBE FERRY.	(ALBION STREET)
	via EGREMONT FERRY.

Liverpool Stage and Moreton,
via SEACOMBE FERRY.

Return Fares.
Liverpool Stage and Leasowe Castle, 8d.
Liverpool Stage and Moreton - - 10d.
(Bermuda Rd. or Leasowe Common—
Pasture Road).
Children Half Fare.

Return Tickets obtainable as follows :
From Liverpool Stage to
Moreton and Leasowe Castle,
At Seacombe Ferry Turnstiles.
From Moreton and Leasowe Castle to
Liverpool Stage,
On Motor Omnibuses.

Liverpool Stage & New Brighton
(ALBION STREET)
via EGREMONT FERRY.

Return Fares.
Liverpool Stage and New Brighton
(Albion Street) ... ... 9d.
Children ... 4d.

Return Tickets obtainable as follows :
From Liverpool Stage to
New Brighton (Albion Street),
At Egremont Ferry Turnstiles.

From New Brighton (Albion Street)
to Liverpool Stage,

On Motor Omnibuses.

AVAILABLE ON DAY OF ISSUE OR FOLLOWING DAY.

This information was taken from a 1932 Wallasey Corporation Time Table and Fares booklet.

48-49 The 1934 buses seem to have been rather camera shy. Leyland TD3 No. 89 is seen at the English Electric works in Preston before delivery in company with a Blackpool Corporation bus with a design of centre-entrance body which Wallasey was soon to try. These buses (Nos.86-91) introduced the large destination indicators which were a feature of Wallasey's buses for the rest of the undertaking's existence. The AEC Regent was the first of six (Nos. 93-98) and is seen in the lower part of Rowson Street, about to turn into Wellington Road. The lamp-mounted bus stop sign was one of several tram stop signs adapted for use by buses by placing a plate inscribed 'Buses' over 'All Cars'. The Regents had fluid flywheels and preselector gearboxes and this one, after being renumbered 193 after the war, was sold to the Manchester bus operator. A Mayne & Sons, for use as spares.
English Electric/C Garner collection

49

50-51 In 1934, Wallasey Corporation experimented with centre entrance buses as used on a large scale at Blackpool. A central staircase split into two and there were power-operated doors. The first to arrive, in April, were two AEC Regents which were mechanically identical with Nos. 93-98. Leyland Titan TD3c No. 92 did not appear until August. This was the first bus in the fleet to be fitted with a torque converter, a form of transmission described by Leyland as 'Gearless'. The centre-entrance buses were all bodied by Charles H Roe Ltd. of Leeds but the seating on the lower deck was awkward and draughts were caused if the doors were left open as they often were.

Charles H Roe Ltd. courtesy R Marshall

51

52-53 The remaining two centre-entrance buses (101-2) appeared in July 1934 and were on the revolutionary AEC 'Q' chassis with side mounted engine. The Roe bodies were of the same general style as the orthodox buses but the weight was so well distributed that single rear wheels were fitted. The model was years ahead of its time and, while there were many single-deckers, including long distance coaches, only 27 double-deckers were built. Birkenhead and Crosville each had one so four ran in Wirral. No. 101 is seen in both views in Victoria Road, New Brighton on a busy summer's day. The seat alongside the driver was especially popular. The Qs were sold in 1943, seeing further service with Yeomans at Hereford, after which both became caravans.
C Garner collection

53

54 The AEC photographer went to Seacombe to catch this line up of the firm's products. Left to right are Nos. 99, 98, 100 and 101. The sleek lines of the Q and the tramcar type lifeguard are well displayed. *AEC Ltd.*

This advertisement was taken from a 1936 Wallasey Corporation Time Table and Fares booklet.

55-56 Two small Leyland Cub KP3 single-deckers with English Electric bodies (12-13), for use on lightly-trafficked services and to replace some ageing Leyland Lions were purchased in 1935. Originally they had only 20 seats (which was then the legal limit for driver-only operation) and a canvas roof which could be wound back in fine weather. They were used on the Promenade and Derby Bathing Pool services and on the No. 9 route from New Brighton to Moreton via Grove Road in the winter months and the No. 7 from Egremont Ferry to Albion Street. When used as one-man buses they attracted public criticism, especially when people had to line up in the rain to pay their fares. They were stored during the war and rebuilt with fixed roofs and 25 seats in 1947, becoming Nos. 5 and 6. Withdrawn in 1950, they both saw further service with Welsh operators.

R Marshall/J P Williams

56

57 This ornate glazed shelter stood on the corner of Grove Road and Warren Drive for the benefit of people changing trams or buses. Note the fading blackout paint on the stanchions and the missing panes of glass - probably the result of air raid damage. Leyland TD4c No. 17 with 1936 English Electric twin-staircase body is showing 'via Martins Lane' on the route indicator as it is working the No. 6 route to Seacombe via Belvidere Road.
Courtesy M Jenkins

58 The first 12 of the open back Leyland Titans (20-31) were withdrawn on 31st December 1935, all being sold to the Scottish operator, W Alexander & Sons Ltd.for whom they ran much longer than in Wallasey. They were replaced by 18 Leyland Titan TD4c buses (14-31) with the familiar twin-staircase English Electric bodywork but eight had their front staircases and doors removed during or just after the war. Seven worked on emergency services in Liverpool in 1941 and ten (22-31) worked for Crosville in Wrexham during the war, some for more than four years. They all had torque converters though No.20 received the engine and transmission from an older bus in 1942. Several were renumbered by adding 100 to their fleet numbers, a common practice in Wallasey in the post-war period when new buses arrived with the same numbers. No. 25 is seen at Seacombe in April 1948. *T G Turner collection*

59

59-60 Wallasey buses on war service. The upper picture shows Wallasey buses in company with London Transport buses in the bus station at the Royal Ordnance Factory, Marchwiel, near Wrexham near the end or just after the war (as the headlamps are unmasked). No. 88, with cream bands painted grey, is on the left and Nos. 24 and 22 (carrying Crosville fleet numbers L424, L422) on the right. The lower picture was taken in the parking ground behind Crosville's Wrexham depot. Six Wallasey buses (including No. 92) are flanked by three ex-Thomas Tilling London Transport Regents on the left and a Crosville Leyland TD7 on the right which had been diverted from Southdown Motor Services in 1940.

Crosville archive

60

61 One of the features of the post-war Wallasey bus service was the extension of the system further into Birkenhead and Bebington. No. 53, a petrol-engined Leyland TD4c of 1937 stands at The Wiend, Higher Tranmere, the usual terminus of the No. 11 route from 1st June 1947. From 1949 to 1956, the buses ran even further at certain times, to the Gorsey Hey Hotel at the end of Teehey Lane, Higher Bebington. The stop sign, in chocolate and cream was the typical Birkenhead sign of the 1930s   *T Davies*

62 The 1939 replacement order went to AEC who supplied six of these Regents (63-68) with the now standard Metropolitan-Cammell bodies. Economics had won the day and these buses were powered by A173 7.7 litre diesel engine with preselector gearbox. No more petrol-engined double-deckers were purchased. They originally seated 52 passengers but two additional seats were placed in the lower deck in November 1942 and two more upstairs in February 1948. They were renumbered 163-8 in 1951 and withdrawn the following year, being sold back to the bodybuilder.   *J P Williams*

63 The new buses for 1937 broke away from the dual-entrance twin-staircase design and set the standard for the next 14 years. The Leyland TD4c chassis were identical to those of the 1936 buses but the handsome Metropolitan-Cammell all-metal bodies set a new standard of elegance. Note the ferry closure blind. There were 24 of these buses, (32-55) all fitted with torque converters; the last two which did not enter service until 1st February, had diesel engines which were much more economical than petrol engines but local amenities were placed before economics and a further order for seven identical vehicles in 1938 (56-62) reverted to petrol power. The 1937 order replaced all the open staircase Leylands which, with the exception of No. 33, migrated to Scotland for many more years' service.
MCW

64 The four Leyland Cubs with 25-seat Burlingham sunshine roof coach bodies (1-4) were bought in 1939 and carried the official party for the opening of the extension of Kings Parade from the Red Noses to Wallasey Beach. They were stored during the war and worked the Promenade and Derby Bathing Pool services after the war and later ran on the 6 and 15 routes at quiet times. The Town Tour started running in August 1952 and was popular for a few years being eventually replaced by a Wirral Tour. They were withdrawn in 1952, Nos. 1 and 2 becoming mobile shops.
T G Turner collection

65 Wallasey was fortunate to take delivery of nine new Leyland TD7c diesel buses in July 1940, just before the air raids started. They were the last to have torque converters and No. 73 was fitted with a gearbox in 1944, giving it a distinctive transmission noise. Numbered 69-77, they nominally replaced 1932 TD2s and Daimlers of the same numbers but, because of wartime conditions, these remained in stock and on one occasion, two No. 71s were seen, the one following the other, in Brighton Street. The Daimlers were sold to Hull Corporation to replace similar buses lost in air raids. No. 70 is seen in Virginia Road where the "cattle pens" have been roofed. The poster on the back advertises Fireworks every Wednesday at New Brighton Bathing Pool. On the No. 17 queue there is a sign warning that the fare to Seacombe on this indirect route is 4d compared with 3d on the Seabank Road route.

T G Turner collection

This advertisement was taken from a "Wallasey Corporation Buses and Ferries Time Table and Fares" for 1939

66

67

66-67 Decorated or illuminated trams and buses were popular to commemorate great events. The coronation of King George VI in 1937 was celebrated by building this striking vehicle using the cab and chassis of 1929 Leyland TD1 No. 33, the only one of its class which did not see further service in Scotland. It was broken up for spares during the war, its engine and gearbox being fitted in TD4 No. 20. After the war, an illuminated bus was made from Lion No. 8, the body of which remained more or less intact beneath the superstructure. Together with No. 7, it was sold to Morris and Pulford, contractors, as a site office in November 1954 and eventually parts of it were used in the restoration of a similar vehicle by Ribble Motor Services Ltd. *T G Turner collection*

68 The first post-war buses were virtually identical to their predecessors of the 1930s. The Leyland PD1 had a larger radiator and a 7.4-litre diesel engine. The new buses arrived in 1946 and were numbered 78-101 though 78-80 were renumbered 108-110 in 1952. Note the advertisement holder on the offside of the cab, a most unsuitable place. It was used mainly to advertise band concerts in Vale Park and similar events. Full size advertisements started to appear on buses in the early 1950s when it became impossible to ignore any source of revenue. A second batch of identical buses (11-34) arrived in 1948.
T G Turner

69

69-70 In the post-war era Wallasey buses carried workers engaged on refurbishing the Mauretania in Gladstone Dock and the work of conveying dock workers continued during the 1950s. No. 88, a 1946 Leyland PD1 with Metro-Cammell body, is seen at Gladstone Dock with an aircraft carrier in the background. In the lower view four Leyland PD1s approach Seaforth Sands station with the Liverpool Overhead Railway structure on the left. No. 11 was the first of the 1948 PD1s.
N N Forbes

70

71 One of the new post-war joint routes with Birkenhead Corporation ran between New Brighton and Arrowe Park via Poulton Bridge and Upton. It was extended to Woodchurch in 1952 and further into the estate two years later. PD1 No. 19 is seen in Virginia Road, New Brighton. These were the last buses to have offside destination indicators. Fleet numbers tended to be applied in different positions in the 1950s, those at the rear often giving place to advertisements.
M Jenkins

72 After withdrawal between 1957 and 1960, several of the 1946 Leyland PD1s were exported to Yugoslavia. Some ran unrebuilt but at least two had the rear end converted for running on the right hand side of the road. This one, still with advertisement frame on the cab, was photographed in Mostar in 1965.
M Jenkins collection

73

74

73-74 The final 24 buses with the 1937 style Metropolitan-Cammell bodies (35-58) were placed in service in 1951. They differed from their predecessors in having sliding windows and no offside destination equipment. They were Leyland Titan PD2/1 chassis with the more powerful 9.8-litre O.600 Leyland engine. In the upper picture, No. 41 stands in Seabank Road at the Trafalgar Road terminus of the part-day joint service 13 to King's Square, Birkenhead, the first regular service to use the Four Bridges. Note the upper destination blind with red lettering on a white ground to draw attention to the fact that it was a part-way point. St Columba's Church, since demolished, is in the background. In the lower picture, No. 50 passes No. 51 in Stringhey Road, Egremont on the Seacombe to New Brighton Station route No. 15 (formerly No. 5).

T G Turner/M Jenkins

75 The roadway at the Derby Bathing Pool terminus originally had a steep camber, restricting it to single-deck buses only but, in 1949, it was regraded and double-deck buses could be safely used. Buses ran through from Seacombe on routes 2 and 6 at very busy weekends but most of the time passengers had to change to the shuttle service 20 which started at the top of Harrison Drive. No. 50 now with a front fleet number stands at the terminus wrongly displaying 'via Belvidere Road'.
N A Eames

76-77 Two views of bus No.54? These pictures demonstrate the extraordinary long life of this design of Metropolitan-Cammell bodywork which Wallasey Corporation adopted as standard. The bus in the top picture, seen in Virginia Road, was a Leyland TD4c and entered service on 1st February 1937 together with identical No. 55 both of which were diesel-powered, a rarity in Wallasey at that time. In March 1951, this No. 54 became No. 154 when the bus in the lower picture arrived. But to some extent it lived on as its diesel engine went into No. 103 and the rest, propelled by 103's old petrol engine was sold to Ribble Motor Services who mounted its body on a wartime Guy Arab utility bus, scrapping the remains. The other No. 54 was a Leyland PD2/1, the main visual difference being the sliding windows. It passed to Merseyside PTE in 1969, was renumbered 254 in 1971 and, after withdrawal in 1972, was purchased by Mr C. Greenwood who restored it to original condition and maintains it in working order. It is at present housed in the Birkenhead Transport Museum in Pacific Road.
S N J White/T G Turner

76

77

78 In 1947, four of the Leyland TD4c buses of 1936 which had been working at Wrexham during the war, had their English Electric double-deck bodies scrapped and were fitted with luxurious coach bodies, being renumbered 7-10. There were 29 well-upholstered seats on a chassis which normally seated 33 passengers. They often worked excursions to Blackpool and elsewhere on hire to Hardings but No. 8 (formerly 27) is seen working the shuttle service between the top of Harrison Drive and Derby Bathing Pool.
R F Mack

79 A further six of the 1936 TD4c buses were given new Burlingham double-deck bodies in 1949 and renumbered 102-7. No. 105 (formerly 25) is seen at Seacombe ferry loading for route 6 with another of the same type on route 15 just beyond it. The torque converters, by now a source of trouble because of shortage of spare parts, were replaced by crash gearboxes but the petrol engines were retained. However, in 1951, Nos. 103-4 received the diesel engines from Nos. 154-5. These same engines went into coaches 9 and 10 when the bodies of 102-7 were transferred to new PD2 chassis in 1955-56.
J P Williams

80 When buses started to run to Moreton Shore in 1931, they displayed the same route number as the main Moreton service - No. 4. This was changed to 4A in 1933 and when 4A was needed for a variation of the main service in 1949, the curious number 4S was coined for the special buses. The Corporation had an aversion to using the term 'Shore' and nearly always called it 'Foreshore' on the buses and 'Leasowe Common' in the timetables. No. 103 has now had its 1949 Burlingham body transferred to a new 1955 Leyland PD2/10 chassis and is seen parked up at Seacombe, erroneously showing 'via Seabank Road'. Seacombe railway station is in the background.

R F Mack

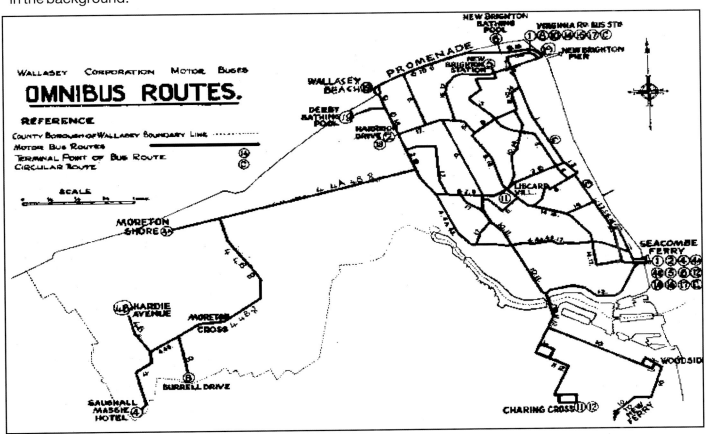

This Omnibus Routes Map was taken from a 1947 Wallasey Corporation Motor Buses 'Fares and Stages' booklet. (We apologise for the poor quality of the original).

81

81-82 Two of the 1948 Burlingham coach bodies (Nos. 7-8) were transferred to new Leyland PD2/10 chassis in 1957 and the upper picture shows No. 8 on its new chassis and No. 9 still on its 1936 TD4 chassis. Note the extra width of the post-war radiator and the alterations to the cab front resulting in the loss of the destination indicator. Following an accident between Nos. 43 and 39 at Lloyds Corner in March 1959, No.8's body was transferred to the PD1 chassis of No. 89 (and renumbered 82 as shown in the lower picture) while EHF 392 became No.43. The coach body was therefore on its third chassis! All the coaches 7-10 were renumbered 81-84 in 1959 to make way for new Atlanteans. *T G Turner/R F Mack*

82

83 Wallasey's first 8ft wide buses with Weymann bodies on Leyland Titan PD2/12 chassis (Nos. 59-70) are lined up behind the depot for photography. Note the two column route number blinds which could show any number from 1 to 99 and single numbers with A, B or S. When No. 10A was introduced there was a problem and '10' was added to the end of the roll.

T B Maund collection

84 A contrast between narrow and wide buses. Before the 1939-45 war, 7ft 6in was the maximum legal width for buses. During the war 8ft wide buses, diverted from overseas orders, were allowed to run under a dispensation and operators and manufacturers campaigned for this to be made permanent. After a transitional period, the 8ft width was legalised in 1950 and Wallasey's first wide buses came in 1951. No. 73 was from the identical 1952 batch - a Leyland PD2/12 with 56-seat Weymann body. It is shown in 1963 with mudguards painted green experimentally but they were repainted black after about a month. The 1949 Burlingham body of No. 104 seems to be wearing well after 14 years' service on two different chassis.

T G Turner

85 Eight-footer No. 72 is awaiting passengers for Saughall Massie. Note the sliding cab door and an advertisement being displayed in the strange offside frame. Buses for Birkenhead were always banished to a stand round the corner in Birkenhead Road and a blue Birkenhead Corporation bus has just left for Charing Cross.

T B Maund collection

86 In 1964, Leyland PD1 No. 127 (ex-27) was converted to a replica of the cruise boat Royal Iris, originally to undertake publicity tours. However, it was used on the Promenade service for a time, by this time numbered 84. It was sold for preservation but it is feared to have been scrapped.

R Marshal

87 This was once a familiar sight at Seacombe ferry with several buses arriving simultaneously and passengers streaming into the ferry terminal. In line abreast are PD2s Nos. 59 and 72 and PD1 No. 33. Seacombe Ferry Hotel, in the background, was noted for its excellent catering.
B. McCann courtesy M Jenkins

This advertisement was taken from a 1960s New Brighton & Wallasey guide.

88

89

90

88-90 The rear-engined Leyland Atlantean was a revolutionary design when exhibited at the 1958 Commercial Motor Show, Wallasey Corporation being the first to operate the type anywhere when No. 1 entered service on 8th December 1958. The Atleanteans seated 77 passengers compared with 56 in the earlier types and their introduction enabled many peak hour duplicates to be withdrawn. Some were run as one-man buses for a time with the upper deck closed off, before double-deck driver-only operation was generally adopted. The pictures show the three different liveries carried. Upper: No. 2 in Virginia Road finished in traditional style with the now rather archaic 'Motors' title. Centre: No. 28 in the 'intermediate' style without the title and with fleet numbers in Gill Sans characters and Lower: No. 25 in the final style which was applied to the fleet generally from 1962.

J P Williams/T G Turner collection

91

92

91-92 Faced with declining traffic, the Corporation experimented with new routes into residential areas for which small buses were needed and acquired four Albion Nimbuses (31-34) with 31-seat bodies by Strachan. The first two entered service on 12th November 1962 on route 23 between Gorsedale Road and Green Lane; it was later extended to Ross Avenue, Leasowe. These buses were also used on routes 6 and 15 at quiet times. When delivered, the Nimbuses were finished mainly in cream with primrose green window surrounds but the colours were reversed on repaint. The lower picture shows No. 31 undergoing the statutory tilt test before delivery. Single-deck buses had to tilt to 35 degrees; double-deckers to 28 degrees.

R F Mack/M Jenkins collection

93 Wallasey can claim to have introduced the minibus to Merseyside as early as 13th May 1963 when another service designed to penetrate residential areas in depth commenced using this second-hand Trojan 13-seater (No.100). Route 22 originally ran from Martins Lane (Grosvenor Street) to New Brighton Station but was eventually curtailed to run between Liscard Village and Kirkland Road with a 6d (2°p) flat fare. The Trojan had a mechanically-operated door and a Perkins diesel engine.
R F Mack

94 In 1967, the Trojan was replaced by this Bedford J2 with 19-seat Duple Midland body. No. 99 is seen turning out of Kirkland Road into Dalmorton Road. By this time Route 22 had been extended from Liscard to Harrison Drive via Broadway Avenue. The Bedford had a six-cylinder petrol engine and was the last bus to be bought by Wallasey Corporation.
M Jenkins

95 The last bus to be painted in Wallasey's traditional livery was Merseyside PTE's Leyland Atlantean 1789. In 1979, ten years after the separate municipal undertakings had ceased to exist, the PTE painted some buses in the liveries of the constituents. 1789, seen here on route 8 at Newton, near West Kirby, retained its livery for five years, long after all the others had been repainted in PTE colours.
R L Wilson

96

97

96-97 No trace now remains of Wallasey's impressive bus garage in Seaview Road, an ASDA supermarket having been built on the site. The steel-framed building in the foreground, was opened in May 1929; it had unobstructed floor space of 18,000 sq.ft. and a clear span of 127 ft. In the background is the former tram depot, pairs of the narrow arches having been knocked into one to facilitate manoeuvring. A section of the interior of the new garage is shown in the lower picture.

T G Turner collection

51

Inside the image:
SEATING CAPACITY 56
UPPER SALOON 30
LOWER SALOON 26

98-99 The standard lower deck interior layout of the Metropolitan-Cammell bodied buses which dominated the Wallasey scene for many years with the brown, ribbed, leather cloth seats which were so familiar to passengers. Above is a 7ft. 6in. wide PD2 while the view of No.69 opposite shows the added spaciousness of the 8ft. wide bodies.
Weymanns Ltd. courtesy M Jenkins

99

100 Birkenhead Corporation with considerable competition from the Mersey Railway offered cheap bus and ferry return tickets on all stages and all routes. Wallasey, with only limited rail competition, issued them only from Moreton and Leasowe where they were in competition with Birkenhead Corporation. This board was erected at Moreton Shore terminus showing that the return fare to Liverpool was 10d (a little more than 4p) or 8d from Leasowe Castle. It is inscribed 'The buses pass through pleasant country and residential areas', inviting comparison, perhaps, with Birkenhead's drab industrial mien. At whom the message was directed is not clear, as most people boarding buses here were on their way home and had already bought their tickets. Birkenhead, with a frequent daily service to Moreton Shore throughout the year, compared with Wallasey's seasonal service, always carried the lion's share of the traffic.

D S Deacon

SUMMARY OF WALLASEY CORPORATION BUS FLEET 1920-69

KEY TO BODY TYPE CODE

B = Saloon Bus, H = Highbridge type double deck L = Lowbridge type double deck
C = Single deck coach DP = Dual purpose vehicle (coach seats in bus body). Figures denote seating capacity, upper deck first.
   Final letter denotes entrance position. F = Front, FD = Front with closing doors, R = Rear, RO = Rear with open staircase, C = Centre and D = Dual. TR = Toastrack.
Note:-HF Registration numbers. Only odd numbers were used for four-wheeled vehicles
   until October 1934 after which even numbers were filled up from HF 4402.

Fleet No.	Registration No.	Chassis Make and Type	Body Make	Type & Capacity	Year in Service	Year Withdrawn	Note
1-6	HF 589-99	AEC Y (Tylor)	E & A Hora	B32R	1920	1926	P
7-10	HF 1737-43	AEC Y (Tylor)	E & A Hora	B32R	1922	1926	Q
1-5	HF 4109-17	Leyland Lion LSC1	Leyland	B31R	1926	1935	
6-7	HF 4531-3	Leyland Lion PLSC1	Leyland	B31F	1926	1935-44	
8-10	HF 4535-9	Leyland Lion PLSC1	Leyland	B31R	1927	1941	
11	HF 4919	Karrier JKL	Hall Lewis	B31TR	1927	1939	
12-3	HF 4923-21	Karrier WL6	Hall Lewis	B40D	1927	1931	R
14-9	HF 5337-47L	Karrier DD6	Hall Lewis	H36/30R	1928	1931	R
20-5	HF 5349-59	Leyland Titan TD1	Leyland	L27/24RO	1928	1935	
26-49	HF 5851-97	Leyland Titan TD1	Leyland	L27/24RO	1929	1935-6	
50-5	HF 6033-43	Leyland Titan TD1	Leyland	L27/24RO	1929	1936	
56	HF 6069	AEC Regent 1	Short	H26/24RO	1929	1938	
57-9	HF 6701-5	Leyland Titan TD1	Davidson	H27/21D	1930	1938	
60-2	HF 6707-11	Daimler CF6	Davidson	H27/21D	1930	1938	
63-4	HF 7435-7	AEC Regent 1	Park Royal	H26/24R	1931	1939	
65-8	HF 7439-45	Leyland Titan TD1	Eastwood & Kenning	H27/21D	1931	1939	
69-71	HF 7857-61	Leyland Titan TD2	English Electric	H27/21D	1932	1946-8	
72-4	HF 7863-7	Daimler CP6	English Electric	H27/21D	1932	1941	
75-77	HF 8253-7	Leyland Titan TD2	English Electric	H27/21D	1933	1948	NZ
78-80	HF 8259-63	Leyland Titan TD2	English Electric	H27/21D	1933	1946	
81-5	HF 8435-43	Daimler CP6	English Electric	H27/21D	1933	1941-2	
86-91	HF 9175-85	Leyland Titan TD3	English Electric	H27/21D	1933-4	1946-8	YZ
92	HF 9381	Leyland Titan TD3c	Roe	H29/23C	1934	1946	
93-8	HF 9383-93	AEC Regent 1	English Electric	H27/21D	1934	1946-8	
99-100	HF 9395-7	AEC Regent 1	Roe	H29/23C	1934	1946	
101-2	HF 9399-401	AEC Q	Roe	H28/28C	1934	1943	
12-3	HF 5008-10	Leyland Cub KP3	English Electric	B20F	1935	1949	T
14-31	HF 5224-58	Leyland Titan TD4c	English Electric	H27/21D	1936	1948-9	UYZ
32-55	HF 6208-54	Leyland Titan TD4c	Metro-Cammell	H28/26R	1937	1950-1	VZ
56-62	HF 7268-80	Leyland Titan TD5c	Metro-Cammell	H28/26R	1938	1950-1	
63-8	HF 8180-90	AEC Regent 1	Metro-Cammell	H28/26R	1939	1952	
1-4	HF 8656-62	Leyland Cub KP4	Burlingham	DP25F	1939	1952-3	
69-77	HF 9116-32	Leyland Titan TD7c	Metro-Cammell	H28/26R	1940	1951-2	
78-101	HF 9574-9620	Leyland Titan PD1	Metro-Cammell	H30/26R	1946	1957-60	W
11-22	AHF 189-200	Leyland Titan PD1	Metro-Cammell	H28/26R	1948	1961-2	X
23-34	AHF 361-72	Leyland Titan PD1	Metro-Cammell	H28/26R	1948	1961-2	X
35-58	AHF 831-54	Leyland Titan PD2/1	Metro-Cammell	H30/26R	1951	1965-72	W
59-70	BHF 45-56	Leyland Titan PD2/12	Weymann 8ft	H30/26R	1951	1968-73	
71-80	BHF 490-9	Leyland Titan PD2/12	Weymann 8ft	H30/26R	1952	1971-4	
102-7	CHF 561-6	Leyland Titan PD2/10	Burlingham	H30/26R	1955-6	1965	U
7-8	EHF 391-2	Leyland Titan PD2/10	Burlingham	C29F	1957	1966	UW
1-6	FHF 451-6	Leyland Atlantean PDR1/1	Metro Cammell	H44/33FD	1958-9	1973-8	
7-20	HHF 7-20	Leyland Atlantean PDR1/1	Metro Cammell	H44/33FD	1960	1973-7	
21-30	JHF 821-30	Leyland Atlantean PDR1/1	Metro Cammell	H44/33FD	1961	1974-9	
31-4	LHF 31-4	Albion Nimbus NS3AN	Strachan	DP31F	1962	1972-4	
100	601 SPA	Trojan	Trojan	B13F	1963	1966	M
99	DHF 162E	Bedford J2SZ10	Duple Midland	B19F	1967	1975	

NOTES

L Not consecutive; 18 was HF 5343 and 17 was HF 5345.

M Ex-Banstead Coaches, Ltd. Banstead, Surrey.

N 77 renumbered 77A 11/41, then 11 late 1945 and 177 late 1946.

P 2-3 renumbered 8-9 in March 1926, following delivery of new buses.

Q Purchased from Liverpool Corporation and re-registered from KB 1968-9/73/9.

R Three-axle vehicles.

T Rebuilt as B25F 1947 and renumbered 5-6.

U 14, 22-3, 25-6 rebodied by Burlingham H30/26R 1949 and renumbered 102-7. Bodies transferred to new chassis 1955-6. 24,
    27-9 rebodied by Burlingham C29F 1948 and renumbered 7-10. Bodies of 7-8 transferred to new chassis 1957. 9-10 renumbered
    83-4 in 1959.

V 32-53 had petrol engines. 54-5 had diesel engines.

W Body of 89 scrapped in 1959. Coach body from 8 (EHF 392) mounted on chassis in 1959. EHF 392 received body
    from 43 the chassis of which was scrapped. 78-80 were renumbered 108-110 in December 1952.

X 27 received body in form of replica of Royal Iris cruise ship in 1963 and renumbered 84.

Y TD3s 86-88, 90-91 and TD4c 14-19, 21 & 28 rebuilt as H31/25R by removing front staircases and entrances in 1944-45.

Z No. 58 (HF 6703) was the experimental coal-gas powered bus 1936-38 and at various times between 1940-44 buses 20, 35, 47,
    77A, 86 & 87 operated on coal gas or naphtha fuel.

From time to time from 1940, buses were retained after their replacements had arrived and 100 was added to their fleet numbers
from 1946 onwards.

---

*This advertisement for Wallasey Corporation buses was taken
from a Holiday Guide for Wallasey & New Brighton dated 1928.*

TICKETS

Many older readers will remember the colourful tickets carried in a rack by the conductor who punched a hole with a Bell Punch. This showed the stage to which the passenger had paid.

1. 3°d grey single ticket punched for an inward journey in stage number 12.

2. For many years, the most expensive ride from Seacombe ferry was 5d (just over 2p) to Bermuda Road, Moreton for which this pale yellow ticket was issued.

3. From 1st December 1930, workmen's return tickets were issued on buses leaving a terminus up to 7.40am at single fare for the return journey, minimum 2d. Officially these were available only to 'artisans, mechanics and daily labourers' but they tended to be issued indiscriminately to any who asked for them. The blue 2°d ticket would give about 5˜ miles of travel for the equivalent of just over 1p.

4. Birkenhead Corporation issued throughbus and ferry return tickets on all their routes but Wallasey, having less railway competition, was less generous. However, they had to equal Birkenhead's facilities between Moreton and Liverpool with a 10d ticket from Bermuda Road or the Shore and an 8d from Leasowe Castle (later from the station). The 10d ticket was yellow, a red stripe indicating a ticket issued on a bus and a green stripe showing that it had been issued at the ferry.

5. A unique facility was a concessionary fare to Unemployed Allotment Holders to reach their gardens at Beaufort Drive and Leasowe Road. There were 1d, 1°d and 2d tickets, this one being white with a red overprint.

6. By the 1960s, the 10d return had increased in stages to 2/6d (12°p), relaxation of restrictions on return date of travel having simplified the layout. This ticket was plain white.

7. Free travel was given to leg-disabled ex-servicemen after the 1914-18 war. The first concessions to people over 70 were not given until 1930 when, for the month of July only, they could travel free between 10.00am and 12 noon and 2.00pm and 4.00pm.

8. After the 1939-45 war, ticket issue gradually became mechanised. These two pink 1°d tickets were issued from an "Ultimate" dispenser, the stage number being printed on issue.

1	2	3	4

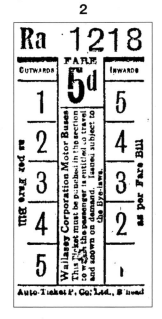   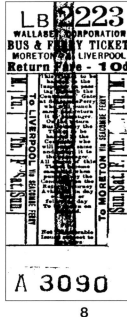

5	6	7	8